I0781418

The Worlds of H.G. Wells: A Biographical Journey

Herbert George Wells, known to the world as H.G. Wells, was a literary visionary who laid the foundation for modern science fiction. Born on September 21, 1866, in Bromley, Kent, England, he would go on to become one of the most influential and prolific writers of the 20th century. Wells' early life was marked by both adversity and curiosity, factors that would shape his future as a writer and thinker.

Wells' parents, Joseph and Sarah Wells, were working-class individuals who struggled to make ends meet. Young Herbert faced financial hardships and health issues, including a significant injury to his leg that left him bedridden for a period of time. However, this confinement provided him with ample opportunity to read and explore the worlds contained in books, a pursuit that would ignite his imagination and set the stage for his literary career.

Wells attended Thomas Morley's Commercial Academy, a local school in Bromley, where he developed a passion for science and literature. His early exposure to the writings of Charles Darwin, Thomas Huxley, and Jules Verne, among others, deeply influenced his thinking and instilled a lifelong fascination with the possibilities of science and the wonders of the natural world.

After completing his formal education, Wells worked as a teacher, a role that provided him with a foundational understanding of education and the challenges faced by the working class. However, it was not long before he decided to leave teaching behind, in order to learn more about principles and methodology of education. Upon finishing this course, Wells turned to journalism in order to earn an income and support himself. During this period, he wrote numerous articles and pieces for various publications, allowing him to hone his writing skills and explore a range of topics. This transition from teaching to journalism served as a crucial stepping stone in Wells' journey toward becoming a prolific writer of science fiction, social commentary, and political advocacy.

In 1895, he published his breakthrough work, "The Time Machine," his first novel that launched his career as a science fiction author. This marked the beginning of a remarkable period of creativity during which Wells would produce a series of groundbreaking novels, including "The War of the Worlds," "The Invisible Man," and "The Island of Dr. Moreau."

A Closer Look at His Notable Works

THE TIME MACHINE (1895): "The Time Machine" is a seminal novella that introduces readers to the concept of time travel. In the story, an unnamed protagonist, often referred to as the Time Traveller, invents a machine that enables him to journey through time. His first voyage takes him to the distant future, where he encounters two distinct races: the Eloi, gentle and childlike, and the Morlocks, subterranean and sinister. Wells uses this narrative as a vehicle to explore the evolution of humanity and to express his concerns about social and scientific progress. The novella's significance lies in its foundational role in shaping modern science fiction, particularly in its use of time travel as a central theme.

THE WAR OF THE WORLDS (1898): "The War of the Worlds" is one of H.G. Wells' most renowned and enduring works. It unfolds a gripping tale of Martian invaders wreaking havoc on Earth with their advanced technology. The story focuses on an unnamed protagonist's experiences as humanity must find ways to survive and resist the extraterrestrial threat. Beyond its thrilling narrative, the novel contains a powerful subtext, implicitly critiquing British imperialism and exploring the vulnerability of humanity in the face of technologically superior forces. The work's exploration of the consequences of unchecked progress has made it a classic in the science fiction genre.

THE INVISIBLE MAN (1897): In "The Invisible Man," Wells tells the story of a scientist named Griffin who discovers a way to become invisible. As Griffin struggles to control his newfound power, he descends into madness, becoming a menace to society, committing crimes, and causing chaos. The novel explores themes of scientific ethics and the moral decay of the protagonist, offering a thought-provoking examination of the consequences of unchecked power. Wells' portrayal of the psychological and moral challenges faced by an invisible character has left an indelible mark on the genre.

THE ISLAND OF DR. MOREAU (1896): "The Island of Dr. Moreau" follows the shipwreck survivor Edward Prendick, who finds himself on an isolated island where the enigmatic Dr. Moreau conducts grotesque experiments to transform animals into human-like creatures. Prendick must navigate the horrors of the island and its disturbing inhabitants. This novel delves into profound ethical questions, touching on themes of morality, the boundaries of scientific experimentation, and the consequences of tampering with nature. It serves as a cautionary tale, raising questions about the blurred lines between humanity and the animal kingdom.

Social and Political Advocacy, War, and Futurism

Beyond his contributions to literature, H.G. Wells was a vocal advocate for social and political change. He was deeply interested in socialism and authored several books on the subject, including "Anticipations" and "The New World Order." He believed in the power of education and the need for a more equitable society. His ideas had a significant influence on the political thought of his time and contributed to the emergence of the modern welfare state.

Wells' concerns extended to global conflicts, and he used his platform to speak out against the devastating impact of World War I. He authored "The War That Will End War" in 1914, a collection of essays that called for an end to militarism and a united effort to prevent future conflicts. Although his hopes for a lasting peace were

dashed by the outbreak of World War II, his
writings continued to inspire generations
of peace activists.

Wells' interest in the future of humanity also
led him to coin the term "atomic bomb" in his 1914
novel, "The World Set Free." This term would later
become synonymous with the destructive power
of nuclear weapons.

Wells passed away on August 13, 1946, leaving
behind a legacy of imaginative storytelling,
social and political advocacy, and a lasting
impact on the fields of science fiction and
futurism. His work remains essential reading for
those interested in the intersection of science,
literature, and the human condition. H.G. Wells'
ability to foresee the consequences of scientific
and technological advancements is often seen as
prophetic. His ideas about the future of
humanity, social reform, and the potential for
destruction and salvation were both thought-
provoking and influential. In the years since
his passing, H.G. Wells' influence continues to
endure, ensuring that his name remains
synonymous with visionary thought and the
limitless possibilities of the human
imagination.

Major Ideas and Philosophy of H.G. Wells

SOCIAL COMMENTARY AND CRITIQUE: H.G. Wells
possessed a sharp social conscience and used his
writing as a platform to criticize and challenge
various aspects of British society during the
late 19th and early 20th centuries. He was

particularly critical of the stark class distinctions that characterized the era, where extreme wealth and privilege existed alongside dire poverty and squalor. Wells saw these disparities as unjust and unsustainable and often depicted them in his works, urging readers to consider the consequences of such inequality.

He also took aim at British imperialism, exposing the negative impacts of unchecked colonial expansion and its implications on both the colonizers and the colonized. His novel "The War of the Worlds," for instance, can be interpreted as a critique of British colonialism, with the imperialists themselves facing invasion and subjugation by a more advanced civilization.

SCIENTIFIC AND TECHNOLOGICAL FORECASTING: One of Wells' most notable talents was his ability to foresee the implications of scientific and technological advancements. He wrote with uncanny foresight about concepts like time travel, space exploration, and genetic engineering. For example, "The Time Machine" introduced the idea of time travel long before it became a scientific theory. Wells' anticipation of technological developments contributed to his reputation as a visionary writer.

GLOBAL PERSPECTIVE: H.G. Wells held a strong global perspective, advocating for international cooperation and peace as a means to prevent future global conflicts. He envisioned a world in which nations would set aside their differences and unite under a single governing body, often referred to as a "World State." He believed that such unity would not only prevent wars but also facilitate the equitable distribution of resources and promote the welfare of all humanity. Wells' global vision was an early form of what today is often referred to as global governance or world federalism, where the goal is to create a global political authority to address international issues and conflicts.

UTOPIAN AND DYSTOPIAN VISIONS: Wells was a prolific author of both utopian and dystopian fiction. In works like "The Time Machine" and "The War of the Worlds," he presented contrasting visions of humanity's future. "The Time Machine" offered a glimpse of a divided future, with the Eloi representing a utopian society and the Morlocks embodying a dystopian one. This dichotomy allowed Wells to explore the potential for both progress and decay within human society.

THE HUMAN CONDITION: Throughout his writings, Wells grappled with profound questions about the human condition. He probed the depths of human nature, contemplating our capacity for both good and evil. He explored the influence of science and technology on the human experience, reflecting on our power to shape the world and our responsibility in doing so. His works often encouraged readers to ponder the moral and ethical dimensions of scientific progress and the consequences of our actions.

SECULAR HUMANISM: Wells leaned towards secular humanism, a philosophical and ethical stance that emphasizes reason, ethics, and compassion without the influence of religion. He championed the idea that humans should take responsibility for their own destiny and well-being without relying on religious dogma or supernatural beliefs. This perspective aligns with his views on progress, education, and social reform, which were all based on human agency and the potential for individuals and societies to improve through rational and ethical decision-making.

PROGRESSIVE IDEAS: Wells was a prominent proponent of progressive ideas, advocating for social, political, and economic change. He aligned with socialist principles and believed in the need for a more balanced distribution of wealth and resources within society. He saw socialism as a means to address the economic disparities and injustices he observed in British society during his lifetime. Wells' progressive ideals encompassed not only economic reform but also the promotion of education, women's rights, and universal access to knowledge.

ENVIRONMENTAL CONCERNS: In his science fiction works, particularly "The War of the Worlds" and "The Time Machine," Wells raised important ecological and environmental concerns. He used his stories to highlight the consequences of environmental neglect and the potential long-term impacts of humanity's actions on the planet. In "The War of the Worlds," the invading Martians wreak havoc on Earth's ecosystems, illustrating the vulnerability of our environment to external threats. In "The Time Machine," Wells explored the far future where humanity's disregard for the environment had dire consequences. These themes served as early warnings about the need for environmental stewardship and the potential consequences of unsustainable practices.

EDUCATION: H.G. Wells held a deep appreciation for education as a cornerstone of societal improvement. He believed that intellectual curiosity and the pursuit of knowledge were fundamental to human progress. Wells saw education as a means to uplift individuals and society as a whole. He promoted the idea that access to education should be widespread and not limited by social class or economic status. His belief in the power of education aligns with his broader vision of social reform and a more equitable and just society.

H.G. Wells' ideas and philosophies were interconnected, reflecting his desire for a more peaceful, just, and intellectually enlightened world. His global perspective, secular humanism, progressive values, environmental concerns, and emphasis on education collectively demonstrate his commitment to addressing social and moral challenges and to shaping a more promising future for humanity. H.G. Wells' ideas and philosophies were interconnected, reflecting his desire for a more peaceful, just, and intellectually enlightened world. His global perspective, secular humanism, progressive values, environmental concerns, and emphasis on education collectively demonstrate his commitment to addressing social and moral challenges and to shaping a more promising future for humanity. This book of quotes from H.G. Wells' various works aims to present his thoughts and ideas in a compact form and encourage further exploration.

Face this world.
Learn its ways, watch
it, be careful of too
hasty guesses at its
meaning. In the end
you will find clues
to it all.

The whole human
memory can be, and
probably in a short
time will be, made
accessible to every
individual.

Find the thing you want
to do most intensely,
make sure that's it,
and do it with all your
might. If you live, well
and good. If you die,
well and good. Your
purpose is done.

Civilization is in a
race between education
and catastrophe. Let us
learn the truth and
spread it as far
and wide as our
circumstances allow.
For the truth is the
greatest weapon
we have.

It is a law of nature we overlook, that intellectual versatility is the compensation for change, danger, and trouble. An animal perfectly in harmony with its environment is a perfect mechanism. Nature never appeals to intelligence until habit and instinct are useless. There is no intelligence where there is no change and no need of change. Only those animals partake of intelligence that have a huge variety of needs and dangers.

If we do not end war –
war will end us.
Everybody says that,
millions of people
believe it, and
nobody does
anything.

How small the
vastest of human
catastrophes may
seem at a distance
of a few hundred
miles.

Heresies are
experiments in
man's unsatisfied
search for truth.

A federation of all
humanity, together
with a sufficient
measure of social
justice, to ensure
health, education,
and a rough equality
of opportunity to
most of the children
born into the world,
would mean such a
release and increase
of human energy as to
open a new phase in
human history.

New and stirring
things are belittled
because if they are
not belittled the
humiliating question
arises, 'Why then are
you not taking part
in them?'

Books -- bright
windows in this life
of ours, lit by the
shining souls of
men.

We live in a
world of unused
and misapplied
knowledge
and skill.

Patriotism has become
a mere national
self assertion,
a sentimentality of
flag-cheering with no
constructive duties.

We were making the
future and hardly any
of us troubled to think
what future we were
making. And here it is!

A time will come when
men will sit with
history before them or
with some old newspaper
before them and ask
incredulously,
"Was there ever
such a world?"

An animal may be
ferocious and cunning
enough, but it takes a
real man to tell a lie.

Advertising is
legalized lying.

It is the going out
from oneself that is
love and not the
accident of its
return. It is the
expedition, whether
it fail or succeed.

Every respectable citizen of the
professional classes passes through a
period of activity and imagination,
of "liveliness and eccentricity,"
of "Sturm und Drang." He shocks his
aunts. Presently, however, he realizes
the sober aspect of things. He becomes
dull; he enters a profession; suckers
appear on his head; and he studies.
Finally, by virtue of these he settles
down—he marries. All his wild
ambitions and subtle aesthetic
perceptions atrophy
as needless in the presence of calm
domesticity. He secretes a house, or
"establishment," round himself, of
inorganic and servile material. His
Bohemian tail is discarded. Henceforth
his life is a passive receptivity to what
chance and the drift of his profession
bring along; he lives an almost entirely
vegetative excrescence on the side of a
street, and in the tranquillity of his
calling finds that colourless
contentment that replaces happiness.

And I have by me, for my
comfort, two strange
white flowers...to
witness that even when
mind and strength had
gone, gratitude and a
mutual tenderness
still lived on in
the heart of men.

There has been ... an enormous waste of human mental and physical resources in premature revolutionary thrusts, ill-planned, dogmatic, essentially unscientific reconstructions and restorations of the social order, during the past hundred years.

The science hangs like
a gathering fog in a
valley, a fog which
begins nowhere and
goes nowhere, an
incidental, unmeaning
inconvenience to
passers-by.

The British Islands are small islands and our people numerically a little people. Their only claim to world importance depends upon their courage and enterprise, and a people who will not stand up to the necessity of air service planned on a world scale, and taking over thousands of aeroplanes and thousands of men from the onset of peace, has no business to pretend anything more than a second rate position in the world. We cannot be both Imperial and mean.

Why had we come to the moon?
The thing presented itself to me
as a perplexing problem. What
is this spirit in man that urges
him for ever to depart from
happiness and security, to toil,
to place himself in danger,
to risk an even a reasonable
certainty of death? It dawned
upon me that there in the moon
as a thing I ought always to
have known, that man is not
made to go about safe and
comfortable and well fed and
amused. ... against his interest,
against his happiness, he is
constantly being driven to do
unreasonable things. Some force
not himself impels him, and he
must go.

Dragging out life
to the last possible
second is not living
to the best effect.

An artist who
theorizes about his
work is no longer
artist but critic.

A time when all such
good things will be
for all men may be
coming more nearly
than we think. Each
one who believes that
brings the good time
nearer; each heart
that fails delays it.

The path of social
advancement is and
must be strewn with
broken friendships.

If you do not want
to explore an egoism
you should not read
autobiography.

A time will come when
a politician who has
willfully made war and
promoted international
dissension will be as sure
of the dock and much surer
of the noose than a private
homicide. It is not
reasonable that those who
gamble with men's lives
should not stake
their own.

Our minds fall very readily under the spell of such unmitigated words as Purity and Chastity. Only death beyond decay, absolute non-existence, can be Pure and Chaste. Life is impurity, fact is impure. Everything has traces of alien matter; our very health is dependent on parasitic bacteria; the purest blood in the world has a tainted ancestor, and not a saint but has evil thoughts.... This stupidity, this unreasonable idealism of the common mind, fills life to-day with cruelties and exclusions, with partial suicides and secret shames. But we are born impure, we die impure; it is a fable that spotless white lilies sprang from any saint's decay, and the chastity of a monk or nun is but introverted impurity. We have to take life valiantly on these conditions and make such honour and beauty and sympathy out of our confusions, gather such constructive experience, as we may.... Life is that, and abstinence is for the most part a mere evasion of life.

When the mind
grapples with a great
and intricate problem,
it makes its advances
step by step, with but
little realization of
the gains it has made,
until suddenly, with
an effect of abrupt
illumination, it
realizes its victory.

Adapt or perish,
now as ever,
is nature's
inexorable
imperative.

Man is an
imperfect animal
and never quite
trustworthy in
the dark.

Few people realise
the immensity of
vacancy in which the
dust of the material
universe swims.

Man is the unnatural
animal, the rebel
child of nature, and
more and more does he
turn himself against
the harsh and fitful
hand that reared him.

But I was too restless
to watch long; I'm too
Occidental for a long
vigil. I could work at
a problem for years,
but to wait inactive
for twenty-four
hours - that's
another matter.

Even men who were engaged
in organizing debt-serf
cultivation and
debt-serf industrialism
in the American cotton
districts, in the old
rubber plantations,
and in the factories of
India, China, and South
Italy, appeared as
generous supporters of
and subscribers to the
sacred cause of
individual
liberty.

With wine and food,
the confidence of
my own table, and
the necessity of
reassuring my wife,
I grew by insensible
degrees courageous
and secure.

A strange persuasion
came upon me that, save
for the grossness of the
line, the grotesqueness
of the forms, I had here
before me the whole
balance of human life
in miniature, the whole
interplay of instinct,
reason, and fate in its
simplest form.

I saw great and
splendid architecture
rising about me, more
massive than any
buildings of our own
time, and yet, as it
seemed, built of
glimmer and mist.

Marriage isn't what
it was. It's become a
different thing
because women have
become human beings.

There is no more
evil thing in this
world than race
prejudice, none at
all. [...] It justifies
and holds together
more baseness,
cruelty, and
abomination than
any other sort of
error in the world.

What good is religion
if it collapses under
calamity? Think of what
earthquakes and floods,
wars and volcanoes,
have done before to men!
Did you think that God
had exempted [us]? He is
not an insurance agent.

Nothing endures, nothing is precise and certain (except the mind of a pedant), perfection is the mere repudiation of that ineluctable marginal inexactitude which is the mysterious inmost quality of Being. Being, indeed! - there is no being, but a universal becoming of individualities, and Plato turned his back on truth when he turned towards his museum of specific ideals.

Science is a match that man has just got alight. He thought he was in a room - in moments of devotion, a temple - and that his light would be reflected from and display walls inscribed with wonderful secrets and pillars carved with philosophical systems wrought into harmony. It is a curious sensation, now that the preliminary splutter is over and the flame burns up clear, to see his hands and just a glimpse of himself and the patch he stands on visible, and around him, in place of all that human comfort and beauty he anticipated - darkness still.

Crude
classifications and
false generalisations
are the curse of all
organised human life.

Until a man has found God
and been found by God, he
begins at no beginning,
and works to no end.
He may have friendships,
his partial loyalties,
his scraps of honor. But
all these things fall into
place and life falls into
place only with God. Only
with God. God, who fights
through men against Blind
Force and Night and Non-
Existence; who is the end,
who is the meaning. He is
the only king.

We are always getting
away from the present
moment. Our mental
existence, which are
immaterial and have
no dimensions, are
passing along the
Time-Dimension with
a uniform velocity
from the cradle
to the grave.

I was never a great amorist, though I have loved several people very deeply.

Our true nationality is mankind.

Crime and bad lives
are the measure of a
State's failure, all
crime in the end is
the crime of the
community.

I was no longer very
much terrified or very
miserable. I had, as it
were, passed the limit
of terror and despair.
I felt now that my life
was practically lost,
and that persuasion
made me capable of
daring anything.

The history of India for many centuries had been happier, less fierce, and more dreamlike than any other history. In these favorable conditions, they built a character - meditative and peaceful and a nation of philosophers such as could nowhere have existed except in India.

The professional
military mind is by
necessity an inferior
and unimaginative
mind; no man of high
intellectual quality
would willingly
imprison his gifts
in such a calling.

Strength is the
outcome of need;
security sets a
premium on
feebleness.

All men, however
highly educated,
retain some
superstitious
inklings.

Fools make researches
and wise men exploit
them...and we thank
Heaven for an assumed
abundance of
financially impotent
and sufficiently
ingenious fools.

Looking at these stars
suddenly dwarfed my own
troubles and all the
gravities of
terrestrial life.
I thought of their
unfathomable distance,
and the slow inevitable
drift of their movements
out of the unknown past
into the unknown future.

We should strive to
welcome change and
challenges, because
they are what help us
grow. With out them we
grow weak...in comfort
and security. We need
to constantly be
challenging ourselves
in order to strengthen
our character and
increase our
intelligence.

We do not want
dictators, we do not
want oligarchic
parties or class rule,
we want a widespread
world intelligence
conscious of itself.
To work out a way
to that world brain
organization is
therefore our primary
need in this age of
imperative
construction.

Rest enough for the individual man, too much and too soon, and we call it death. But for Man, no rest and no ending. He must go on, conquest beyond conquest. First, this little planet and its winds and ways. And then all the laws of mind and matter that restrain him. Then the planets about him, and, at last, out across immensity to the stars. And when he has conquered all the depths of space, and all the mysteries of time, still he will be beginning...

The only true measure
of success is the ratio
between what we might
have done and what we
might have been on the
one hand, and the thing
we have made and the
things we have made of
ourselves on the other.

I'm a damned fool, sir.
Because I've reservoirs
and reservoirs of muscular
energy, and one or other
of them is always leaking.
It's a most interesting road,
birds and trees, I've no
doubt, and wayside flowers,
and there's nothing I should
enjoy more than watching
them. But I can't. Get me on
that machine, and I have to
go. Get me on anything, and I
have to go. And I don't want
to go a bit. Why should a man
rush about like a rocket,
all pace and fizzle? Why?
It makes me furious.

We are living in 1937, and our
universities, I suggest, are not half-
way out of the fifteenth century.
We have made hardly any changes
in our conception of university
organization, education, graduation,
for a century - for several centuries.
The three or four years' course of
lectures, the bachelor who knows some,
the master who knows most, the doctor
who knows all, are ideas that have come
down unimpaired from the Middle Ages.
Nowadays no one should end his
learning while he lives and these
university degrees are preposterous.
It is true that we have multiplied
universities greatly in the past
hundred years, but we seem to have
multiplied them altogether too much
upon the old pattern.. [A] new
university is just another imitation
of all the old universities that have
ever been. Educationally we are still
for all practical purposes in the coach
and horse and galley stage.

If you are in
difficulties with a
book, try the element
of surprise: attack it
at an hour when it
isn't expecting it.

Humanity either
makes, or breeds,
or tolerates all
its afflictions,
great or small.

Satan
delights equally
in statistics
and in quoting
scripture...

Statistical
thinking will one
day be as necessary
for efficient
citizenship as the
ability to read
and write.

There's nothing wrong
in suffering, if you
suffer for a purpose.
Our revolution didn't
abolish danger or
death. It simply made
danger and death
worthwhile.

Every man shall be
entitled to a sound and
objective education and
there shall be genuine
equality of opportunity.
Education shall be a
matter of environment as
well as of instruction,
and everyone shall be
entitled to an education
untouched by the
interests of any party
or religion.

Every one of these
hundreds of millions of
human beings is in some
form seeking happiness....
Not one is altogether
noble nor altogether
trustworthy nor
altogether consistent;
and not one is altogether
vile.... Not a single one
but has at some time wept.

Armament should be an illegality everywhere, and some sort of international force should patrol a treaty-bound world. Partial armament is one of those absurdities dear to moderate-minded 'reasonable' men. Armament itself is making war. Making a gun, pointing a gun, and firing it are all acts of the same order. It should be illegal to construct anywhere upon earth any mechanism for the specific purpose of killing men. When you see a gun it is reasonable to ask: 'Whom is that intended to kill?'

In England we have
come to rely upon a
comfortable time lag
of fifty years or a
century intervening
between the perception
that something ought to
be done and a serious
attempt to do it.

Perhaps I am a man of exceptional moods. I do not know how far my experience is common. At times I suffer from the strangest sense of detachment from myself and the world about me; I seem to watch it all from the outside, from somewhere inconceivably remote, out of time, out of space, out of the stress and tragedy of it all. This feeling was very strong upon me that night. Here was another side to my dream.

It is the system of
nationalist individualism
that has to go....We are
living in the end of the
sovereign states....In the
great struggle to evoke
a Westernized World
Socialism, contemporary
governments may
vanish....Countless
people...will hate the new
world order....and will die
protesting against it.

Every time I see an
adult on a bicycle,
I no longer despair
for the future of
the human race.

It is possible to believe
that all the past is but
the beginning of a
beginning, and that all
that is and has been is
but the twilight of the
dawn. It is possible to
believe that all the
human mind has ever
accomplished is but
the dream before the
awakening.

There is, though I do
not know how there
is or why there is,
a sense of infinite
peace and protection
in the glittering
hosts of heaven.

Beauty isn't a
special inserted
sort of thing. It
is just life, pure
life, life nascent,
running clear
and strong.

[The] restoration of
the past is one of the
most astonishing
adventures of the
human mind.

The Boss: You are not
mechanics, you are
warriors. You have
been trained, not to
think, but to do.

Phase by phase these ill-adapted governments are becoming uncontrolled absolutisms; they are killing that free play of the individual mind which is the preservative of human efficiency and happiness.

The fertilising
conflict of
individualities
is the ultimate
meaning of the
personal life.

I hate and despise a
shrewish suspicion
of foreigners and
foreign ways; a man
who can look me in
the face, laugh with
me, speak truth and
deal fairly, is my
brother, though his
skin is as black as
ink or as yellow as an
evening primrose.

Life begins perpetually. Gathered together at last under the leadership of man, the student-teacher of the universe... unified, disciplined, armed with the secret powers of the atom, and with knowledge as yet beyond dreaming, Life, forever dying to be born afresh, forever young and eager, will presently stand upon this earth as upon a footstool, and stretch out its realm amidst the stars.

The weaving of mankind
into one community does
not imply the creation of
a homogeneous community,
but rather the reverse;
the welcome and adequate
utilization of
distinctive quality
in an atmosphere of
understanding...
Communities all to one
pattern, like boxes of toy
soldiers, are things of
the past, rather than of
the future.

There is no reason
whatever to believe
that the order of
nature has any greater
bias in favour of man
than it had in favour
of the ichthyosaur or
the pterodactyl.

The forceps of our
minds are clumsy
forceps, and crush
the truth a little in
taking hold of it.

I believe that the
crazy combative
patriotism that
plainly threatens to
destroy civilisation
to-day is very largely
begotten by the
schoolmaster and the
schoolmistress in
their history lessons.
They take the growing
mind at a naturally
barbaric phase and
they inflame and fix
its barbarism.

Great and strange ideas transcending experience often have less effect upon men and women than smaller, more tangible considerations.

We live in reference
to past experience
and not to future
events, however
inevitable.

I had just taken to
reading. I had just
discovered the art of
leaving my body to sit
impassive in a crumpled
up attitude in a chair or
sofa, while I wandered
over the hills and far
away in novel company
and new scenes... My
world began to expand
very rapidly,.... the
reading habit had
got me securely.

Ashoka (264 to 227 B.C.), one of the great monarchs of history, whose dominions extended from Afghanistan to Madras... is the only military monarch on record who abandoned warfare after victory.

Science has toiled
too long forging
weapons for fools to
use. It is time she
held her hand.

The true strength of
rulers and empires
lies not in armies or
emotions, but in the
belief of men that they
are inflexibly open and
truthful and legal.
As soon as a government
departs from that
standard it ceases to be
anything more than 'the
gang in possession,' and
its days are numbered.

To ride a bicycle
properly is very like
a love affair-chiefly
it is a matter of faith.
Believe you do it, and
the thing is done;
doubt, and, for the
life of you, you
cannot.

The cat, which is a
solitary beast, is
single minded and
goes its way alone,
but, the dog, like his
master, is confused
in his mind.

Leaders should lead
as far as they can and
then vanish. Their
ashes should not
choke the fire
they have lit.

Very much indeed of what we call moral education is such an artificial modification and perversion of instinct; pugnacity is trained into courageous self-sacrifice, and suppressed sexuality into religious emotion.

On the supposition that the world is to go on divided among aggressive sovereign states, with phases of war preparation known as peace and acute phases of more and more destructive war, it is quite a good move in the game. On the supposition that the world is growing up to an age of reason, and that a world of civilisation is attainable, it is a monstrous crime.

The Athenian
democracy suffered
much from that
narrowness of
patriotism which
is the ruin
of all nations.

But there are times when
the little cloud spreads,
until it obscures the
sky. And those times I
look around at my fellow
men and I am reminded
of some likeness of the
beast-people, and I feel
as though the animal is
surging up in them. And I
know they are neither
wholly animal nor holy
man, but an unstable
combination of both.

Every citizen knows
his place. He is born
to that place, and the
elaborate discipline
of training and
education and surgery
he undergoes fits him
at last so completely
to it that he has
neither ideas nor
organs for any
purpose beyond it.

Money means in a thousand minds a thousand subtly different, roughly similar, systems of images, associations, suggestions and impulses.

If I am something of a
social leveller, it is
not because I want to
give silly people a
good time, but because
I want to make
opportunity universal,
and not leave out one
single being who is
worth while.

A day will come when
beings, now latent
in our thoughts and
hidden in our loins,
shall stand upon
Earth as a footstool
and laugh, and reach
out their hands
amidst the stars.